RONALD REAGAN

A Life From Beginning to End

Copyright © 2017 by Hourly History.

All rights reserved.

Table of Contents

Introduction
The Small Town Boy
Reagan's Hollywood Career
The Political Stage
The Governor's Race
Reagan's Hat in the Ring
The Assassination Attempt
Reagan and the Evil Empire
The Alzheimer's Diagnosis
The Reagan Legacy

Introduction

The 40th president of the United States, Ronald Wilson Reagan, came to 1600 Pennsylvania Avenue by way of the silver screen and perhaps no president was more adept at embodying the image of the United States as a country made up of heroes. Reagan had made his mark as a sportscaster and an actor; he came to politics after success in occupations which seemingly had nothing to do with governing. But when he was an actor, he served as president of the Screen Actors Guild, an introduction to leadership that would expand hugely after he paid his dues in politics.

The most successful leaders are those who enter the pantheon of myth after a career spent bending destiny their way and Reagan was no exception. He had known hard times in his life, but struggle never embittered him. His love of country sometimes blinded him to the means used to achieve desired ends, but he pursued his goals with single-minded dedication that never became bogged down in the conservative ideology that could have led to hostility between the parties. Reagan was willing to work with savvy Speaker of the House Tip O'Neill in order to bring about legislation; the current polarization of the political parties in Washington D.C. makes many Americans long for the days when Democrats and Republicans were patriots with different views and not the bitter enemies that they seem to be today. He was the first president to come to the White House with a divorce in his past, but he and First Lady Nancy Reagan lived a love affair that made their romance another part of the Reagan legend.

As America wrestles with intransigent political stances, burgeoning threats from home and abroad, and a newly-elected president whose unpredictability raises global alarm, who can blame them for hearkening back to the Reagan years? How would the man who took on the Soviet Union have handled the Russia that has evolved since the Cold War ended? How would he address the barrier between Democrats and Republicans and inspire them to work for the good of the country rather than their own political stances?

What can we, and our leaders, learn from the lessons of the 40th president, Ronald Reagan?

Chapter One

The Small Town Boy

"We can't help everyone, but everyone can help someone."

—Ronald Reagan

Jack Reagan, a shoe salesman with a talent for telling stories and a weakness for alcohol, was the grandson of an Irish immigrant named Michael O'Regan who left Ireland for London and then made his way to Carroll County, Illinois in 1856. O'Regan had already changed his name to Reagan before he arrived in the United States, so when his son, John Michael Reagan, and his wife became parents in 1883, they passed the family name onto their son, who became known as John Edward "Jack" Reagan. In 1904, Jack Reagan married Nelle Wilson, the oldest of the seven children of her Scottish-English parents, who lived in a farming town on the Illinois prairie.

It was far from uncommon for women to give birth at home at that time, and sons Neil, born in 1908, and Ronald, born on February 6, 1911, arrived in a second-floor apartment of a commercial building in Tampico, Illinois, just one of the many towns in which the wandering Reagans would live. But after her second son, Ronald Wilson Reagan, who would earn the nickname "Dutch" because, according to his father, he resembled a fat little Dutchman, was born, Nelle Reagan was advised not to have more children.

Times were hard for the family. The Reagan family traveled to other towns in Illinois, following the jobs for Jack Reagan, who only had a grade-school education. During the years of Ronald's childhood, the family was also dealing with Jack's drinking. One episode where his father had passed out in the snow and the young Reagan had to drag him back inside, left a painful imprint on the boy, who forever recalled what it was like to live with an alcoholic father. In 1919, they returned to Tampico and lived above the H.C. Pitney Variety Store, until 1920, when the store closed and the family settled in Dixon, Illinois.

Despite the close ties that Reagan would feel for his small town home, Dixon, Illinois had, like many other small towns in early twentieth-century America, a streak of racial discrimination in the people; the local inn refused to allow African-Americans to spent the night there. When Ronald Reagan learned this, he brought the people home where his mother had them spend the night and served them breakfast the next morning. His father's social conscience also left a mark on Ronald Reagan, as Jack Reagan refused to allow his sons to see the popular movie *Birth of a Nation* because of the favorable light in which the Ku Klux Klan was portrayed. Reagan was raised with a deeply rooted belief in the equality of the races, a view which would be challenged by society in the twentieth century as African-Americans sought their rightful place in the nation's establishment.

The Reagans knew difficult times and their finances were strained, but poverty didn't diminish Nelle Reagan's spirit. Her husband was a Roman Catholic, but Nelle's religious faith provided her with the spirit that she needed to endure life's struggles, and as a member of the Disciples of Christ Church, she taught Sunday school and led in readings of the Bible during the religious services. And when the pastor wasn't in town for the midweek services, it was Nelle who led the prayers. Nelle was a woman who sought and saw the best in other people, with religious beliefs that shaped the woman that she was and the way she raised her children. Nelle Reagan's Protestant beliefs influenced her son, and Ronald followed his mother's path of faith and was baptized in the Disciples of Christ Church in 1922.

He may have been as awestruck by his mother's powerful prayer presence as others in the religious communities; the members of her church certainly regarded her with reverence for her resolute faith. A church member whose daughter was ill was told by the pastor that, as a Christian, she needed to be able to accept death. But after the service ended that Sunday and the rest of the congregation had left, Mrs. Mildred Neer noticed that Nelle Reagan was still there, gathering the music that the members had left behind. Mrs. Neer went to Nelle and told her about her child who was ill. Mrs. Reagan suggested that they get on their knees and pray for the four-year old child. They did so, for hours, with Nelle not leaving until 6:00 pm that evening. Not long after that, the abscess on the little girl's neck burst. Mrs. Neer said, "God had heard Nelle Reagan's prayer and answered it."

Nelle's faith was passed on to her son, who said, "I know that she planted that faith very deeply in me." She may also have passed on a talent for acting. She appeared in *The Ship of Faith* in 1926 and received a favorable review, with the critic noting that Nelle Reagan was one of Dixon, Illinois' favorite readers and always pleased the audiences she appeared before. Her thespian talents and her faith created an impressive model for the son who would employ both of those traits in his public life.

As a student at Dixon High School, Ronald Reagan was able to pursue his interests in sports and acting. Known to be a strong swimmer, Reagan found work as a lifeguard in 1927 at the Rock River in Lowell Park; during six years of employment, newspaper reports show that he rescued seventy-seven swimmers during his lifeguard tenure. Following his graduation, Reagan enrolled at Eureka College, a liberal arts school which had a Disciples of Christ orientation. He joined the Tau Kappa Epsilon fraternity, where he washed dishes to help pay for his tuition, some of which was provided by the partial football scholarship he had received. Here Reagan continued to enjoy swimming, working as a lifeguard and a swimming coach and also joining the college swim team.

He sampled student journalism, working on the school newspaper as a reporter and on the yearbook as an editor, and was part of the drama club and the debate club. Some of the money Reaggan earned from his college jobs went back to Dixon to help his family. Reagan's belief in the virtues and rewards of hard work were demonstrated during his early years, where nothing was handed to him, and he had to earn his way. The labor strengthened his self-respect and furnished a foundation for the views he would later hold when he was making decisions on the social programs that the government supported.

But it wasn't all work. Reagan became a cheerleader, and he was captain of the swim team and also played on the football team. His academic record was less successful; he majored in sociology and economics, graduating with a C average. His years at Eureka helped to nurture another aspect of Reagan's formation, as he was introduced to the world of politics. Reagan's political instincts were honed after he was elected president of the student body, where he spearheaded a strike of the students against Eureka's president when the president moved to reduce the number of faculty members. Reagan gave a speech, protesting the elimination of the classes that had been dropped because of the college's financial issues as a result of the Depression. Reagan was effective and successful in his efforts. The president resigned his position after the strike ended.

The Reagans were Democrats, and Franklin D. Roosevelt's election in 1932 was regarded as a promising direction for the nation which was suffering from the worst economic crisis it had ever known. Jack Reagan's support of Democratic politics earned him the position of local director of the Works Progress Administration, one of the programs in FDR's New Deal which was designed to help unemployed Americans get work. The Reagans' son Neil also found work with the WPA. Although Reagan would later switch political affiliations from Democrat to Republican, he continued to regard FDR with admiration for his efforts to save the country during the Great Depression.

In 1932, Reagan graduated from Eureka, but the job market was particularly poor as the Great Depression drove millions of Americans out of work. Eventually, he was able to find employment in Davenport, Iowa as a radio announcer for $10 a game and travel costs. Reagan began to develop the speaking skills that would prove so effective later in his public career. By memorizing only the first line of the commercials that he narrated, he learned that the rest of his spiel sounded more natural. His prowess was quick and within two years, having been promoted to staff announcer, he transferred to an NBC radio outlet in Des Moines.

In Des Moines, he became a baseball announcer for the Chicago Cubs, providing play-by-play coverage using the descriptions of the games that came over the wire while the games were going on. It was a successful gig, and by 1936, Reagan traveled with the team, receiving by now a substantial salary for his work. But that didn't mean that he had stopped seeking ways to better himself and broaden his opportunities.

When the Cubs went to California in 1937, Ronald Reagan took a screen test to see if he had any acting talent. The boy from Dixon, Illinois was about to make his first foray into fame.

Chapter Two
Reagan's Hollywood Career

"They didn't want them good; they wanted them Thursday."

—Ronald Reagan

The 1937 screen test opened the door to a seven-year contract with the "B-film" unit of Warner Brothers Studio. For people who were obliged to count their pennies to make ends meet, movies were an affordable and popular form of entertainment for Americans who were still mired in the Great Depression. A Ronald Reagan screen credit first appeared in 1937 when he had a role in the film *Love is on the Air*, and by 1939, he had 19 films to his credit, including *Dark Victory*, where he appeared with Humphrey Bogart and Bette Davis.

In 1940, he appeared in the movie that would become most closely identified with him when he played the part of George "the Gipper" Gipp in *Knute Rockne, All American*. The story of terminally ill George Gipp and his renowned request to Notre Dame Coach Rockne that, when the football team was struggling, to tell them to "go out there with all they got and win just one for the Gipper" would join the ranks of Reagan legend. It was a slogan and a mantra, and given Reagan's heartfelt belief in the ability to defeat the odds, a creed as well.

His success continued and so did his popularity when, in 1941, he was named the fifth most popular Hollywood star of the younger generation of actors by the movie exhibitors. By now, Nelle had taken on a new role as she took up the job of answering Reagan's fan letters. Reagan expected his career to continue to grow and he played a double amputee in 1942 in *King's Row*, in what he would describe as his favorite role; he said the film made him a star and many critics regarded it as his best film.

But the real world was about to intervene in the make-believe world of acting; on April 18, 1942, two months after *King's Row* was released, Reagan was ordered to active duty. However, Reagan was nearsighted, and his eyesight was poor, classifying him for limited service and unable to join the forces overseas. The film would go on to be nominated for a Best Picture Academy Award, but Reagan's movie career would never recover from the interruption.

Reagan was sent to the San Francisco Port of Embarkation at Fort Mason, California, where he was a liaison officer of the Port and Transportation Office. On May 15, 1942, he applied for a transfer from the cavalry, where he was assigned to the AAF Public Relations. He ended up in the 18th Army Air Force Base Unit, more familiarly known as the First Motion Picture Unit in Culver City, California. The primary film production unit of the US Army Air Forces, this group would go on to produce over 400 propaganda and training films.

After a promotion to first lieutenant in January 1943, Reagan was sent to the Provisional Task Force Show Unit of *This is the Army*, in Burbank, California. He completed the assignment and was promoted to captain in July of the same year. Some of the films that he acted in and narrated included *Recognition of the Japanese Zero Fighter* and *Beyond the Line of Duty*, which won an Oscar for Best Short Film.

Reagan's movie star status was of use to the military, and in 1944, he went to take part in the Sixth War Loan Drive, a campaign encouraging the home front to buy war bonds to help finance the war effort. In November, he returned to his assignment with the First Motion Picture Unit, staying there until war's end in 1945. Although there was a recommendation to promote him to major, the proposal was ultimately denied.

By the time that World War II was over, many men who left military service found a new challenge when they returned home to take up their lives and their careers. This was also true for Ronald Reagan, who before the war was on track to become a major star. The delay, and the years spent out of view from the movie-going public, cost him. By the time the war was over, and he returned to his film career, his momentum was gone and he was no longer on the fast track to stardom. Movie roles continued in films like *Bedtime for Bonzo, John Loves Mary, The Hasty Heart, Hellcats of the Navy* and others, but they were not the kind of films that would relaunch his movie career. However, *Hellcats of the Navy*, while it did not do much for his star status, was a movie that would forever change his life.

Co-starring in the film with Reagan was young actress Nancy Davis. The two had met in 1949 when she contacted Reagan, who was the Screen Actors Guild president, because her name had been confused with that of another Nancy Davis, jeopardizing her career because the name had appeared on a blacklist of alleged communists. This was the era of Joe McCarthy's witch hunt against suspected communist sympathizers, and the label of being a "Red" could destroy an acting career. Reagan was single again, his first wife, actress Jane Wyman having filed for divorce in 1948, and the chemistry between Davis and Reagan was immediate. As she put it, "I don't know if it was exactly love at first sight, but it was pretty close." The couple married in a quickly arranged ceremony on March 4, 1952, with actor William Holden as Reagan's best man. Some, noting that daughter Patti was born eight months later, believed that there was a reason for the haste of the marriage, but the couple had been dating for several years, although Reagan was at first hesitant to remarry after his divorce.

The marriage, which would endure for 52 years until Reagan's death in 2004, would, like so many aspects of his life, become the stuff of legend. When he later became president, Reagan's press secretary noted that the couple never took one another for granted. Writing to her, Reagan once expressed, "Whatever I treasure and enjoy— this home, our ranch, the sight of the sea— all would be without meaning if I didn't have you."

During Reagan's presidency, the two were reported to frequently display their affection for one another, although cynics derided what seemed to many like a saccharine narrative of love. She called him "Ronnie" and he called her "Mommy," and Nancy Reagan unabashedly devoted herself to her husband. The public was accustomed to devoted political wives, but the enraptured stare that Nancy Reagan wore when watching her husband give a speech was mocked as "The Gaze." The Reagans didn't care. They were in love for all the years of their marriage and for them, the fairy tale was real.

Reagan's life was changing. He was a happily married man, but his career no longer promised the great things that he had once hoped for. Reagan's passions were also beginning to change, and despite the fading career, he was discovering a new relevance.

Chapter Three

The Political Stage

"I didn't leave the Democratic Party. The party left me."

—Ronald Reagan

In 1941, Reagan had been elected to the Screen Actors Guild Board of Directors as an alternate member. His military service interrupted his involvement as a political leader in SAG, but when he returned to his civilian life, he also returned to SAG leadership, becoming the union's third vice-president in 1946. His growing interest in politics would have a casualty in his personal life, however.

Reagan had married actress Jane Wyman in 1938 after the two had acted in the film *Brother Rat*. The couple went on to have three children, Christine, who only lived a day, Maureen, and Michael, who was adopted. Wyman was a Republican and Reagan was a Democrat at the time, and their political divide, emphasized by her husband's ambitions to become more politically active and his duties as a member of SAG, strained the marriage and the divorce was finalized in 1949. The fact that Wyman's career was thriving while her husband's was fading may also have played a part in the deterioration of the marriage.

Although no longer married, Wyman and Reagan remained harmonious after their divorce; Wyman would go on to vote for her ex-husband, the first divorced American president, when he ran for national office. As a Democrat during that time, Reagan's politics leaned left, and Warner Brothers Studio had stopped him from taking part in an anti-nuclear rally in Hollywood in 1945. He supported Harry Truman's candidacy for president in 1948 and showed up on stage during a campaign speech.

But the end of World War II and the onset of the Cold War with the Soviet Union had inspired a new political consciousness in Reagan, particularly in his perception that communist influences had infiltrated some of the organizations he had previously supported, such as the Americans Veterans Committee. By 1952, he was supporting Republican candidates for president.

While still married to Jane Wyman, Reagan had supplied the FBI with the names of actors that he believed held communist sympathies. He also testified before the House Un-American Activities Committee, affirming his belief that the nation had to be protected from the threat of Marxist ideology and its growing reach in the world beyond Soviet borders.

Politics seemed to be a new and dynamic niche for the actor. In 1947, following the adoption of conflict-of-interest bylaws in the Screen Actors Guild, Reagan was elected as SAG president following a special election. He would be elected to serve seven terms as their president during a time of political turmoil. Labor and politics have long had a tumultuous relationship in American history.

This was also true for Reagan's SAG presidency, as ramifications of the Taft-Hartley Act, which was seen as the response to the rise of unions in the years immediately after World War II, made themselves known. The business community responded to the increase of labor strikes that lasted four times longer than the strikes that had taken place during the war, and labor unions felt that they were unfairly treated in the new environment.

But Reagan the actor wasn't yet ready to make politics his full-time career. His movie success had faded, but the new medium of television offered a second chance. General Electric hired him to take part as an actor and narrator in a new program known as *General Electric Theater*. The program was a popular feature on the Sunday night lineup. In addition to his role on the program, GE also exploited Reagan's movie fame by sending him to give speeches at its work plants to workers and executives, helping Reagan to perfect his speaking technique.

For Reagan, it was more than a job in the acting field; it was, in many ways, a petri dish for the development of his political ideology. As he met with middle managers who felt that the federal government demanded too much in taxes and had too much power, Reagan's speeches to the GE employees celebrated his concept of freedom and the threat of Big Government. Over the eight years that he worked for GE, Reagan gave speeches to more than a quarter of a million GE employees at all 135 of the company's plants. Traveling by train because he was fearful of flight, he would write his speeches in longhand during the trip and then transfer the text to 3x5 index cards, honing an amiable, folksy speaking style flavored with stories from *Reader's Digest* and local newspapers. These speeches would form the core of his moral convictions and political character, emphasizing the good and the positive while stressing the need for Americans to preserve their freedoms against a government that sought to take them away.

Reagan drew a salary of $150,000 a year until GE canceled his contract in 1962 because he would not comply with plans to revise the format of the show so that it could compete with the new Western in town, *Bonanza*. But his unemployment didn't last; Neil, now an advertising executive, was able to find a new job for his brother as the host of the Western *Death Valley Days*. Reagan was successful, well-paid, and, incidentally, on his way to becoming a Republican.

The Democratic ideology that had enveloped the nation during the Great Depression and World War II was losing momentum. Republicans like Arizona's Senator Barry Goldwater supported the view that the Republican Party needed to be more conservative, focusing its efforts on restricting the power of the central government and stopping the advance of communism. Despite Democratic victories in the 1960 and 1964 election, Goldwater was able to imprint his views on his party.

Helping him in this evolution was Ronald Reagan; in a nationally televised speech supporting Goldwater's candidacy for president in 1964, Reagan rallied support for the Republican goals to limit the federal government's involvement in domestic programs like LBJ's Great Society while expanding the role of the military to battle Soviet aggression.

The Republicans lost to Lyndon Johnson and the Democrats in the election of 1964, but the foundation for the new Republican Party had been built, and one of its standouts would be Ronald Reagan.

Chapter Four

The Governor's Race

"I don't know, I've never played a governor."

—Ronald Reagan

How does a Hollywood actor get to the White House? In Ronald Reagan's case, the best pathway was through the governorship of California. His friends and political allies believed that Reagan, with his winning personality and his commitment to the new face of the Republican Party, had a chance; they hired a political consulting firm, Spencer-Roberts, to guide them in the strategy.

Victory wouldn't come easily. California was governed by two-term Democrat Edmund G. Brown who had defeated well-known Republicans in his previous elections. But California, like the rest of the country in 1966, was in the midst of seismic challenges that frightened the electorate: Vietnam was splitting the country into pro-war and anti-war factions, California's Watts riots of 1965 had become, to some Americans, the face of the civil rights movement, and the counterculture had a home in California that seemed to subvert domestic security.

But Governor Brown didn't take his opponent seriously. Brown was convinced that a candidate whose portfolio consisted of B-movies wasn't a real threat to his political future. He also felt that, because the reaction to Barry Goldwater's presidential campaign had been so adverse due to the senator's right-wing views, Reagan was the easier candidate to beat. A bit of political chicanery involving the leaking of damaging information about the other Republican candidate was intended to help Brown's chances, but the technique didn't work. Reagan won over his opponent, and he made an issue of the domestic budget that Governor Brown had forged, saying that it should be reviewed with fresh eyes. When voters seemed dubious about his ability to turn acting into governance, Reagan was unperturbed; when he was asked about the kind of governor he would be, Reagan genially replied that he didn't know because he'd never played a governor before. People liked his blunt promise: if elected governor, he said that he would send the "welfare bums" back to work and he'd "clean up the mess."

His victory was a triumph, winning 53 of California's 58 counties. Californians who had feared that he would be a rigid conservative found that he was a pragmatist willing to compromise. However, the students involved in the protest movements didn't trust him, and Reagan didn't back down on his insistence that they had to obey the rules. The student protests on the Berkeley campus remained in Reagan's crosshairs.

Reagan took office on January 2, 1967, when the Golden State had what was then its largest budget deficit in its history. Committed to his vow that he planned to cut the state budget, Reagan quickly learned that his intention to cut ten percent across the board wouldn't work, and he had to present one that was more realistic. So, in order to conform to the state constitution requiring a balanced budget, Reagan proposed increases in taxes; he achieved bipartisan support for this plan even though some conservative members of his party opposed him.

Four months into his first term, the Therapeutic Abortion Act was introduced in the California state senate. The purpose of the bill was to end the back-alley abortions which often ended up harming or killing the pregnant mother. Reagan signed the bill into law but later said that he would not have done so had he been a more experienced governor; he later adopted a pro-life stance against abortion.

Nancy Reagan, who had retired from her acting career in 1962 to be a wife and mother to the couple's daughter Patti and son Ronald Junior, was not as content living in Sacramento, the state capital, as she had been in Los Angeles. Four months after moving into the Governor's Mansion, she moved the family, at the Reagans' own expense, into a wealthy suburb, citing statements by fire officials calling the mansion a firetrap. Although the move ignited controversy, Nancy later redeemed herself in the public eye when she was appointed to the California Arts Commission. She also promoted the Foster Grandparents Program, and with her husband, hosted dinners for former Vietnam prisoners of war, visited the handicapped and the elderly, and performed many of the traditional duties of a First Lady. But her primary role, as she saw it, was to provide a comfortable home for her husband where he could find a respite from the political fray.

It was inevitable that Reagan and the student movement would clash. When the People's Park protests against the Arab-Israeli conflict erupted on Berkeley's campus, Reagan sent in the California Highway Patrol. The result was Bloody Thursday; one student was killed, another blinded, and more than one hundred officers were injured. Reagan's response was to call out the California National Guard and assign them to occupy the campus for two weeks. The Guard ended up staying for 17 days while the demonstrations calmed down.

Re-elected to a second term in 1970, Reagan seemed to have hit his stride in the role. The following year saw the passage of the Welfare Reform Act, which established more stringent eligibility requirements, along with increased benefits, for Californians seeking state assistance. Working with Democrats, Reagan was able to send property tax reform to the legislature, even though some conservative members of his party were not happy with the program.

Environmental concerns became a national issue in the 1970s, but Californians were suspicious of Reagan's commitment to ecology because of his support of the business sector. But when he appointed a man who was both a member of the Sierra Club and a lumberman to the position of resources director, Reagan ended up promoting the creation of the Redwood National Park. He opposed the building of a dam that would have had a ruinous effect on California's scenery, and he signed a bill into law that protected California's wild rivers on the northern coast of the state.

Reagan left the governor's office after his second term with an established resume in politics. As early as his first term as governor, he was already gauging his political chances for higher office. In 1968, Reagan was part of the Stop Nixon movement for the presidency; if Richard Nixon and Nelson Rockefeller failed to win enough delegates on the first ballot at the Republican National Convention, Reagan felt that he had a chance to be the nominee. But he ended up in third place; his time would come, but in the meantime, he had a state to run. By the time he had completed his second term as governor, Ronald Reagan was thinking of a future in national leadership.

Chapter Five

Reagan's Hat in the Ring

"Are you better off than you were four years ago?"

—Ronald Reagan

Leaving the governor's office did not mean that Ronald Reagan intended to disappear from view. He began writing a political column that was published in 175 newspapers, where readers could follow his political thoughts, as well as giving speeches and radio commentaries. The 1976 election was guaranteed to be a raucous one; conservatives were still upset with President Gerald Ford, who had become president following the ignominious resignation of Richard Nixon after the Watergate scandal.

Ford had enraged much of the country when he pardoned Nixon. By naming Nelson Rockefeller as his vice president after he replaced Nixon, Ford disregarded the feelings of conservative Republicans who found no favor in the liberal New York former governor. Even when Ford dropped Rockefeller from the campaign ticket in 1976, the damage was done, and Ronald Reagan saw his chance to contest Ford for the Republican nomination.

However, Ford out-strategized Reagan in the New Hampshire primary and six subsequent primaries. But when Reagan countered by making Ford's plan to return the Panama Canal to Panama a campaign issue and accusing Secretary of State Henry Kissinger of being easy on the Soviet Union, Reagan went on to win the North Carolina primary, keeping his campaign alive.

In the end, Ford was named the Republican candidate, albeit by a narrow margin which warned of trouble to follow in the election. By the time Ford lost to Georgian Jimmy Carter in the national election, the Republican Party knew that it had a new leader with the potential to restore it to power.

Reagan was ready for the 1980 election and declared himself a candidate in November 1979. He was not the only Republican who sought the nomination, and at first, it seemed as though the conservative, older Reagan was unlikely to win against prominent, experienced Republicans like Senators Howard Baker and Robert Dole, former CIA director George Herbert Walker Bush, former Texas governor John Connally, and Representatives John Anderson and Phillip Crane. The candidates were cutthroat in their zeal to win the nomination: Bush described Reagan's promise to balance the federal budget, reduce taxes and increase military spending as voodoo economics, a stance also held by John Anderson, who said that the only way Reagan could accomplish these opposing goals was with mirrors.

The candidates had the resumes and the facts, but Reagan had personality. He campaigned for 21 days in a row for the New Hampshire primary, disproving any claims that his age was an impediment to his energy. His vigorous performance in the debates attracted the public's interest, and he ended up winning 21 of the 33 primaries which saw him square off against Bush. When it was time for the convention, Reagan assuaged the fears of the moderate Republicans by naming George H. W. Bush as his vice president for the campaign.

The campaign was unruly. John Anderson had entered the race as a third-party candidate, and both Republican nominee Ronald Reagan and Democrat incumbent Jimmy Carter had reason to fear Anderson's ability to take votes away from them. Ultimately, Reagan's query to the American public helped to influence the decision. "Are you better off than you were four years ago? Is it easier for you to go and buy things in the stores than it was four years ago? Is there more or less unemployment in the country than there was four years ago? Is America as respected throughout the world as it was?" These questions, voiced in the context of the nation's economic woes, focused the voters' attention on what was wrong with their country and Carter's leadership.

Compounding Carter's campaign was the ongoing Iran hostage crisis which seemed to show the United States as weak. On November 4, 1979, Iranian students who supported the Ayatollah Ruhollah Khomeinihad stormed the American embassy in Tehran, taking 52 Americans hostage. A year later, the Americans were still hostages, and many blamed Carter's impotent leadership for the blow to the nation's prestige.

Reagan won 489 electoral votes compared to only 49 for Carter. As feared, John Anderson's candidacy did take votes away from Carter, but Reagan's victory was a landslide, making Carter's loss the worst that had ever been experienced by any incumbent seeking election since Republican President Herbert Hoover, in the depths of the Great Depression, lost to Franklin D. Roosevelt. Reagan's coattails proved triumphant for the Republican Party as well; the GOP won 53 seats in the House and 12 in the Senate.

Assembling a Cabinet that would mesh with his plans while working well together was his first challenge. He chose previous supporters to fill the positions of Attorney General and Secretaries of Labor and Transportation. He gave Richard Schweiker, who would have been his running mate in 1976 had Reagan won the nomination, the position of Health and Human Services Secretary.

But he faced a quandary with his choice for Secretary of State. Caspar Weinberger, who had been Reagan's finance director while he was governor of California, wanted the role. So did George Schultz, whose assets were touted by the members of the Reagan transition team. Reagan ended up naming Alexander Haig, who had been Richard Nixon's chief of staff near the end of the Nixon presidency, and Weinberger ended up as Secretary of Defense.

The Reagan Revolution, as his election was called, was poised to recalibrate the American political agenda. The oldest man up to that time to be elected to the office of president, Ronald Reagan, age 69, brought with him a fondness for the America of myth and a vigor that would transform the federal government. In his inaugural address on January 20, 1981, Reagan explained his philosophy, "In this present crisis, government is not the solution to our problems; government is the problem." He had vowed that he would rein in the federal government's spending while cutting taxes, and reduce the ballooning deficit.

His solutions to the problems of the America's economic, political, and international dilemmas would be bold and transformational, but he was not destined to have a placid introduction to his role as president. He did, however, start his presidency on a high note: after 444 days in Tehran, the American hostages were released on the day that Reagan was inaugurated.

Chapter Six

The Assassination Attempt

"A recession is when your neighbor loses his job. A depression is when you lose your. Recovery is when Jimmy Carter, loses his."

—Ronald Reagan

Working in Reagan's favor was the fact that outgoing President Jimmy Carter had failed to gain traction for his agenda. Carter had come to Washington D.C. proud of his status as a Washington outsider. The Democrats controlled the House of Representatives, but Carter had not made allies of his party members. Reagan didn't plan to repeat that mistake, and while he was the president-elect, he reached out to Democratic Speaker of the House Tip O'Neill to lay the groundwork for a legislative foundation.

But no one, not even the president of the United States, can plan for everything. Reagan had only been president for just over two months when, on March 30, 1981, shots fired by John Hinckley, Jr. struck Reagan, his press secretary James Brady, a Secret Service agent, and a Washington policeman. Reagan didn't realize that the shots had hit and thought his ribs had been broken from when Secret Service agents forced him into the limousine to get him out of the line of fire. But as Reagan started coughing up blood, he was raced to the hospital, stabilized in the emergency room, and subsequently sent to the operating room. His customary humor, even at that grim moment, manifested itself as he explained the shooting to First Lady Nancy Reagan by telling her, "Honey, I forgot to duck!" When on the operating table, Reagan jocularly expressed the wish that all of his doctors were Republicans.

Reagan was lucky; Hinckley's shot missed his heart by less than one inch, making Reagan the first serving U.S. president to survive the shots of an assassination attempt. On April 11, Reagan was well enough to be discharged from the hospital.

The shooting shocked the nation, and Reagan benefitted from the outpouring of support that the electorate showed. The tax and budget cuts passed, with a couple of behind-the-scenes deals to make it work; Reagan promised not to campaign in the mid-term 1982 election against the Southern Democrats, known as the Boll Weevil Democrats, in the House of Representatives if they voted for his tax and budget bills. But the Economic Recovery Tax Act of 1981 wasn't the immediate rescue of the economy that Reagan had anticipated. Unemployment which had been high under Carter hit a peak of 10.8% in December 1982, which was higher than the rate had been at any time since the Great Depression.

The president signed tax increases into law from 1981 to 1987 in order to fund various government programs, including Social Security. But over the years of his presidency, the gross domestic product grew at a rate of 7.9% annually.

Domestic issues continued to occupy his attention. Reagan's leadership was challenged later in the summer of 1981 when the Professional Air Traffic Controllers Organization (PATCO) called an illegal strike that threatened the nation's air transportation system. PATCO had given its support to Reagan when he was a candidate for president, one of the few labor unions to endorse him, but when the 12,000 members of the union defied the back-to-work order, Reagan fired them, leaving the busy nation's air traffic control in the hands of new hires and managers. But the disastrous results that were predicted did not happen. Reagan's reputation as a man capable of making strong decision was reinforced, and his actions emboldened the business world, which sensed that it could deal more firmly, and perhaps ruthlessly, with organized labor.

The year 1983 saw the country experience a welcome economic recovery; the gross national product increased, unemployment went down to 7.4 percent in 1984; inflation was under control, and the Dow Jones industrial average rose almost 33 percent during the first term. Following through on his determination to rebuild the American military, Reagan pursued enormous increases in defense spending which also helped to infuse the economy with growth.

Although Reagan's economic programs brought more Americans out of poverty since World War II had galvanized the economy, there was a disparity in the boom. Rich Americans saw their incomes rise by 9 percent, poor Americans saw average income go down by 8 percent, and child poverty increased above what it had been during the mid-1960s.

As the economy expanded, so did the national debt. The budgets that Reagan sent to Congress were not balanced, and Congress, by adding spending programs, increased the deficit. During Reagan's presidency, the national debt rose from $914 billion to $2.6 trillion.

America's increased spending on defense would yield results besides an increase in the deficit as the Soviet Union, facing its own economic drought, would have to come to terms with its limitations. Pursuing his determination to defeat communism, he ordered an enormous build-up of the military, overseeing the deployment of the Pershing missile in West Germany for NATO, producing the MX missile, and reviving the B-1 Lancer program.

Reagan had a staunch ally in his battle against the Soviet Union. British Prime Minister Margaret Thatcher, the Iron Lady, was just as vehement in her denunciation of the country that Reagan described as an evil empire, the Soviet Union. When Reagan addressed the British Parliament on June 8, 1982, Reagan declared that "the forward march of freedom and democracy will leave Marxism-Leninism on the ash heap of history." A year later, he made the prediction that communism would collapse. Reagan would ultimately be proven correct in his forecasting.

He went into the 1984 presidential campaign well-armed for success, and the nation confirmed his expectations by returning him to the White House for a second term. In his bid for re-election, Reagan won 49 out of the 50 states as his opponent, former Vice President Walter Mondale carried only his home state of Minnesota and Washington D.C. His 525 electoral vote tally was the most of any candidate for the American presidency. With such an overwhelming triumph, Reagan expected to build upon his victories of his first term.

But Reagan in his second term would face enormous challenges, some of which would be internal within his administration. Members of a president's Cabinet often leave after the first term, but in Reagan's Cabinet, the changes would ultimately affect his effectiveness. Howard Baker had left in part because of the internal battles with the conservatives of the administration. William French Smith left the position of Attorney General and was replaced by Ed Meese. Jim Baker accepted the position of Treasury as he and Don Regan switched jobs. The results were mixed; Baker was a success, but Meese found himself in the midst of controversy, and Don Regan felt capable of making decisions without consulting President Reagan first. Nancy Reagan saw the problem in succinct terms, Regan, she said, "liked the sound of chief but not of staff."

There was much work ahead in his second term, but there would also be dissension and scandal at home as Reagan forged ahead to his greatest foreign policy success.

Chapter Seven

Reagan and the Evil Empire

"Peace is not absence of conflict; it is the ability to handle conflict by peaceful means."

—Ronald Reagan

It's impossible to assess Ronald Reagan's views on the Soviet Union and the Cold War without considering his genuine apprehension of the threat of nuclear war. His ultimate goal was for the world to be free of nuclear weapons. But his first Secretary of State Alexander Haig felt that it was his role, not President Reagan's, to set foreign policy. After 18 months, Haig was replaced in the position by George Schultz, who was experienced in government and willing to follow the president's agenda. That meant that relations with the Soviet Union were a priority.

Reagan was convinced that the Soviet Union had failed to keep its word in the SALT II treaty which was intended to keep the nuclear parity between the United States and the Soviet Union. In 1982, he resumed arms talks with the Soviets with the goal of limiting the arms race. Reagan decided that a military build-up would make the point not only to the Soviet Union but also to the European allies. The Soviets, Reagan reasoned, would agree to negotiate.

He told his advisers "Defense is not a budget issue. You spend what you need." The defense budget had already been increased under Carter's administration, but Reagan increased spending even more; seven percent increases from 1981 to 1985 came to almost $1 trillion.

Meanwhile, the Soviets were in the throes of their own internal uncertainty. During Reagan's first term, the Soviets were led by a succession of three different men, which created an inconsistent foreign policy. Reagan, however, was anything but inconsistent. Not only the Soviets needed to be contained, he believed, but so did their various spheres of influence. Of particular concern was the Soviet proxy presence in Central America, which Reagan blamed on Cuba. When he delivered his State of the Union message in 1985, he wanted to rally support for anti-communist forces battling the Soviets and their minions from Afghanistan to Nicaragua, a policy that came to be known as the Reagan Doctrine. The Reagan administration was already at work enforcing his rhetoric with covert military aid to the Contras, the military force in Nicaragua fighting against Daniel Ortega and the Sandinista government.

Mindful of the unpopularity of United States intervention in Latin American countries where a history of meddling in elections and governments had created hostility toward the powerful neighbor to the north, Reagan's most public act was the October 25 invasion of Grenada, a minuscule Caribbean nation, where American students could be in danger because of the murder of the country's leader. Reagan had a more far-reaching motive for the invasion: the Cubans were building a new airport in Grenada, and Reagan was suspicious that the 10,000-foot runway was part of a plan to establish a Marxist beachhead in the Caribbean. The American invasion didn't take long and was a success from the American point of view. Politically, and perhaps cynically, it also served to divert attention away from the October 23 bombing of a marine barracks in Beirut, Lebanon, which killed 241 soldiers during the Lebanese Civil War. The incidents were not unrelated. Terrorists in Lebanon were taking American hostages, and Reagan wanted to win their release.

In 1985, Reagan gave his approval to supply weapons to arch-enemy Iran in order to work for the release of those hostages who were held by Hezbollah, a terrorist organization that gave their loyalty to the Ayatollah Khomeini, the man who had installed an Islamist government in Iran, which had previously been a secular nation. The deal to supply Iran with weapons in exchange for the release of the hostages was covert because it was not in accordance with either the intent of the Congress, which had a Democratic majority, or with the Reagan administration's official policy.

Hearings began in August 1987, when it was learned that the National Security Advisor had authorized the diversion of the money earned from the weapons sales to the Contras in Nicaragua who were fighting against the Sandinista government, doing this without notifying the president of what was going on. The televised hearings riveted the nation as high-ranking government officials like former Defense Secretary Caspar Weinberger and military aide Lieutenant Colonel Oliver North captured headlines.

By 1987, as Reagan's time in office was coming to a close, Nancy Reagan was concerned about her husband's legacy. She sought support in persuading President Reagan to address the issue publicly, and on March 4, 1987, Ronald Reagan gave a speech on television where he accepted responsibility for the scandal.

There were convictions, but eventually, they were overturned, and when Reagan's successor to the presidency, George H.W. Bush, was about to leave office, he pardoned everyone who had been indicted in what came to be known as the Iran-Contra Affair.

That episode was a dismal failure and a low mark in American international policy. However, one of the cornerstones of Reagan's aims seemed promising. After a succession of old, ailing leaders, the Soviet Union in 1985 was under the leadership of Mikhail Gorbachev, who was relatively young at age 54, and who realized that his country's economy could not thrive without reforms. He pursued two dynamic new politics, "perestroika" or restructuring of the economy, and "glasnost" which eased the rigid political structure of the nation. But such policies could only work if there was also a rehabilitation of the relationship with the United States. By spending less on defense, Gorbachev felt that he could use that money to save the Soviet economy.

The two leaders began meeting in November 1985. They did not reach accord, but they did agree to continue to meet. At the 1986 summit in Reykjavik, Iceland, Reagan and Gorbachev both pursued the goal of ridding the world of nuclear weapons, but they disagreed on the process leading to that point. Reagan refused to give way on the "Star Wars" military system that he supported, Gorbachev insisted that this was mandatory. The summit ended, seemingly with no results. Reagan's adamant stance convinced Gorbachev that there would be no yielding. But the Soviets admitted privately that they would be leaving Afghanistan, which had turned into their version of the quagmire that Vietnam had been for the United States before Reagan left office. The negotiations continued.

In December 1987, Mikhail Gorbachev came to Washington D.C. as the two nations continued to work toward common, peaceful goals. The following year, Reagan went to the Soviet Union. The Cold War was not over, but the thawing between the two nations was visible and with it a sense that a new era was dawning. The two men had effected a change in the destiny of history, in no small part because Reagan's flexibility to be open to negotiations with the leader of the nation he had called an evil empire. Both men were willing to take the risks necessary to bring peace between their nations.

Chapter Eight

The Alzheimer's Diagnosis

"I have recently been told that I am one of the millions of Americans who will be afflicted with Alzheimer's Disease."

—Ronald Reagan

Reagan's associates and political network had begun to notice that the president sometimes seemed forgetful. As early as 1981, in his first term, Reagan confused his Secretary of Housing and Urban Development with one of the mayors at a reception. Reporter Leslie Stahl, interviewing Reagan in 1986, noticed that he didn't seem to realize who she was until the end of the meeting. However, his doctors denied that there was any physical or cognitive problem in Reagan's health and James Baker, a former chief of staff, denied that the president slept during Cabinet meetings.

In 1989, Reagan was thrown from a horse, requiring treatment for a subdural hematoma. But in late 1992, his doctors detected signs of Alzheimer's Disease. In 1994, Reagan was diagnosed as suffering from Alzheimer's Disease, the neurological condition which destroys a person's brain cells and severs his connection to his memory and his independence. Reagan disclosed the diagnosis in a letter he wrote to the American people: "I have recently been told that I am one of the millions of Americans who will be afflicted with Alzheimer's Disease . . . At the moment I feel just fine. I intend to live the remainder of the years God gives me on this earth doing the things I have always done . . . I now begin the journey that will lead me into the sunset of my life. I know that for America there will always be a bright dawn ahead. Thank you, my friends. May God always bless you."

The disclosure placed a spotlight on a devastating disorder that ravaged its victims by robbing them of their sense of self. Time passed, leaving Reagan able to recognize only a few people that he had once known well. He continued to be active as long as he could by going on walks and playing golf, and even going to his office. In 2001, he broke his hip in a fall and underwent physical therapy when he returned home.

Reagan seldom appeared in public, his family preferring that he retire from public life. His wife was his protector, explaining to CNN host Larry King that she didn't allow many visitors to see him because he would want people to remember him as he was.

On June 5, 2004, Nancy Reagan released a statement: "My family and I would like the world to know that President Ronald Reagan has died after 10 years of Alzheimer's disease at 93 years of age. We appreciate everyone's prayers." A family funeral was held at the Ronald Reagan Presidential Library, where more than 100,000 mourners viewed his coffin. On June 9, the president's body was flown to Washington D.C. to lie in state, only the tenth president to receive that final honor.

At the state funeral on June 11, world leaders such as Margaret Thatcher, Mikhail Gorbachev, Tony Blair, Prince Charles, and numerous others, including Presidents George H. W. Bush and George W. Bush, paid their respects to the American leader who had had such a lasting effect on the world. Inscribed upon his burial site are the words he lived by, "I know in my heart that man is good, that what is right will always eventually triumph and that there is purpose and worth to each and every life."

Chapter Nine

The Reagan Legacy

"From the strong fortress of his convictions, he set out to enlarge freedom the world over at a time when freedom was in retreat—and he succeeded."

—Margaret Thatcher

Ronald Reagan is remembered for many things: his impact on the conservative transformation of the Republican Party, his role in restoring national pride and for rehabilitating the image of the United States in the world, and perhaps most sweepingly, the part he played in ending the Cold War which had consumed the United States and the Soviet Union since the end of World War II.

Both Gorbachev and Reagan felt that it was the world which benefitted from the end of the Cold War. For Reagan, a stalwart believer in democracy and Western values, the ideology that had governed the United States since its inception was the ultimate victor. Reagan, because of his deeply rooted belief in democracy and his publicly emphasized hostility to the Soviet practice of domination, was yet idealistic enough to believe that change could happen. Perhaps he was the only person who could have worked with Gorbachev, himself a transformational leader, to bring about a resolution that no one could have predicted when Reagan took office in 1981.

Reagan's prediction that the Soviet Union would end up on the ash heap of history proved to be correct. The "evil empire" dissolved as the smaller nations once subjugated by the Soviets declared their independence. The Soviet Union was no more, and the Russian Federation that replaced it could not send in tanks to subdue rebellions in the neighboring countries who had feared it in the past.

That whisper of freedom became a roar. On November 9, 1989, after Reagan had left office, the leader of East Germany's Communist Party gave permission for East Germans to cross the border whenever they chose to do so. And they opted to do so, many of them bringing hammers along to bring down the wall which had divided Berlin.

"Mr. Gorbachev, tear down this wall!" was the challenge issued by United States President Ronald Reagan to Soviet Union leader Mikhail Gorbachev to destroy the Berlin Wall, in a speech at the Brandenburg Gate near the Berlin Wall on June 12, 1987. By 1990, when Reagan was out of office, the process of reunifying East and West Germany into one country began. Angela Merkel, the long-time chancellor of Germany, was born in East Germany and is now regarded as one of the most powerful of all the world's leaders, a tribute to the manner in which Germany has absorbed its past into a solid foundation for its present.

Other nations, formerly under the control of Soviet domination, were able to conduct free elections in which citizens voted for their candidates without fear of Soviet reprisal. Former Soviet satellite nations Albania, Bulgaria, Croatia, the Czech Republic, Estonia, Hungary, Latvia, Poland, Romania, Slovakia, and Slovenia belong to NATO, the North Atlantic Treaty Organization formed after World War II to protect Europe.

In short, Reagan changed the map of Europe with his bold initiatives. His domestic legacy is perhaps more nuanced, with some historians pointing to the increase in the number of homeless Americans and the expanding gap in wealth among Americans, as well as to the ongoing concerns about the budget deficit. Still, Reagan is ranked among the nation's most influential presidents, many regarding him as the most effective president since Franklin Roosevelt.

Just as FDR infused liberal policies into American governance, Reagan shifted the nation's direction toward conservatism. It's often said that Reagan's pragmatic conservatism would be rejected as too liberal by the current members of the Republican Party, although he is the icon of the GOP for his success and his popularity.

Ronald Reagan came to the presidency from the acting profession, and when he began his campaign, he was often derided as a lightweight who lacked the gravitas expected of a world leader. But what those critics may fail to realize is that Reagan's success as a president took root from his ability to communicate his creed to the public and persuade listeners to agree with him. That training came from his acting background and garnered him the nickname "The Great Communicator." He was, as a president, much more than the co-star of a simian in *Bedtime for Bonzo*. His ability to imbue his fellow Americans with the conviction that their nation had been blessed by God with a divine mission was not much different from the eloquence of FDR's fireside chats. Both men believed in the myth of America, but they also were convinced that with America's blessings came responsibilities. They were willing to roll up their sleeves and make their idealism a matter of policy.

Any president who can do the same for the generations to come will follow in the footsteps of Ronald Reagan, one of America's most beloved presidents.

Made in the USA
Columbia, SC
09 August 2024